MW00614859

MORNING Opera

Books by Bart Schneider

Poetry
Water for a Stranger

Fiction
Blue Bossaa
Secret Love
Beautiful Inez
The Man in the Blizzard
Nameless Dame (forthcoming)

MORNING

Opera

POEMS

by

Bart Schneider

Kelly's Cove Press

Berkeley

Many thanks to Dan Coshnear, Lisa Leonard, Jim Moore, and Mike Tuggle, early readers of this book who offered guidance and encouragement. A special thanks to Catherine Durand for her daily inspiration.

The poems "Trane at the Urinal," "Monk's Salt," "You've Changed," and "Bird of Paradise" first appeared in slightly different form in *In Digest*. The poem "Van Morrison at the Greek" first appeared in the *North Bay Bohemian*. Thanks to the editors of those publications.

The first line of the poem "Salt Air" was appropriated from Walt Whitman.

Published by Kelly's Cove Press
2733 Prince Street
Berkeley, CA 94705
www.kellyscovepress.com

Published in the United States of America
ISBN 978-1-61364-339-6

First printing

Cover and interior design: Lynn Phelps

Cover painting: *Reports to the Contrary*, oil on linen, by Chester Arnold (2008). Used by permission.

IN MEMORY OF MY PARENTS:

David Schneider 1918-2005
Geri Schneider 1919-2005

Contents

ELEMENTARY

TWO FATHERS

OPEN EYE

PROBABILITIES

BENEDICTION

ELEMENTARY

THE FLOOD

I cried so much
my first weeks
I was left in a basket
in the front yard.
A few hours later
the flooding began.

My father was the first
to fill sandbags.
He stood atop
a sinking tower
and surveyed
the neighborhood.
Climb to higher ground,
he hollered.

Holy men rowed by
speaking in tongues.
My mother carried me
to the rooftop
and held me
over her head.
I'm told
that in swaddling
I looked like an eight-pound
rain cloud.

When the ark arrived,
my mother,
a postpartum ruin,
was forced to speak.
At first we worried
he wasn't ready for this world.
Now he's taking it over.

MILKING THE KEYS

Before she dressed
she sat in her robe
at the piano,
singing arpeggios
that to his little mind
became a herd
of troubled animals,
their fractured voices
rising to calamity.

He faced her sideways,
as if he were
angling his body
to the waves,
for safety.

There were rare times
in his first years
when she forgot
she didn't want to be
anybody's mother.
Once, she handed him
a Pyrex cup with two fingers
of milk and a dipping rag.

She had her own rag and cup
and taught him the art
of milking the keys.
Dip the corner of the rag in the cup—
don't let it get too damp—
then make little circles
like you're polishing the ivories.

They started at opposite ends
and agreed to meet at middle C.
He was in the upper register
and went at it slowly,
workmanlike.
Once in a while he struck a note,
by accident or on purpose,
and stomped
on the sustaining pedal
His mother laughed.

Then he'd go back to his business,
making small circles
on the ivories,
listening to the unplayed notes,
their dying echoes.
He didn't want
the milking to end.

FINGER PAINTING IN MISS BONE'S

I like everything about it,
from putting on our smocks
in the coatroom
to hunching quietly over the art table
while Miss Bone and the paint monitor
prepare the materials.

I love the blank
white sheet in front of me,
ready to zip Z's for Zorro
across vast acres of cacti
and finger-peak Sierras.

But once the paint arrives,
I turn passionate,
smear gaudy stripes
and strokes that glow:
sun-glazed
slicks of pigment
in gas station puddles.

My mind leaves me.
I look at what I've done
and mutter, *Technicolor.*

Miss Bone,
close to six feet
in her sensible shoes,
crouches in a miracle of compression
and studies my picture,
as if it is a fine thing I've made.

QUICKSAND

Tucked in the front rows
of the Balboa Theater
where uniformed ushers hissed
at us and flashed their deadly lights,
I watched the 25-cent Westerns,
convinced that quicksand
was our greatest danger.

Now, I'm not so sure.
I can't say that being swallowed
in a sinkhole of mud
is a fate I'd welcome,
and yet the oblivion
that awaits us,
our final suffocation,
may not offer so regal
a departure.

Imagine going down
atop your faithful steed,
extending your sightless hand
from the pit,
three fingers wriggling
a final prayer.

RITARD

In band class
I loved
when the
whole hulking
mechanism
saw the *ritard*
coming,
shifted down,
and offered
a tight
tremor
of vibrato,
as if it were
tenderness
we were after.

Lucky Chickens

My mother
won a rotisserie
in a bank raffle.
She claimed it
as the only evidence
of luck in her life.
All these years later
it's odd to think
of those big birds,
whose fat
was rendered
during lurching
orbits on the spit,
as lucky chickens,
but that is what
she called them.

NE'ER-DO-WELLS

My mother assigned them
to the darkest circle of Hell.
Oh, what a ne'er-do-well,
she'd say, dismissing
neighbors of small ambition,
or losers riddled with misfortunes
they brought on themselves.

She taunted me about becoming one
and claimed I'd end up with the winos
on Third and Howard.
I'll put money on it.
How much? I growled.
You ne'er-do-well.

One early morning in my twenties
I passed through that neighborhood
just after the street cleaners had pushed
all the pint bottles from the night before
to the curbs. Thunderbird and Ripple,
a nice collection of Night Train.
Not a man or woman to be seen,
but the curbs were swollen
with this crystal majesty.

I was glad to see the ghosts of the ne'er-do-wells,
but a bit sorry to have missed their party.

AUNT LILLIAN

When I was fourteen,
maybe fifteen,
she asked what I planned
to do with my life.
We'd know by now
if you were a genius.

I shrugged behind
the Sporting Green.
So, you're a work
in progress, she said,
and showed me the proper folds
for reading a newspaper
while eating my eggs.

She delivered them poached,
and I, disguised as a gentleman,
partook of them with buttered toast,
the world neatly framed
in the *Chronicle.*

In high school,
long-haired and disheveled,
I'd visit her.
She'd feed me pot roast and pose
philosophical queries,
challenge the sanctity
of my adolescent rebellion.

Are you thinking for yourself
or simply wearing the uniform
of nonconformity?
I told her that I'd never before
been where I was.
Well, then, she said,
you'd better keep going.

FOREIGN FILMS

At sixteen
I walked the beach
from Kelly's Cove
to the Surf Theatre
convinced that growing
up by the ocean
was good breeding
for an existentialist.

Even the Surf's lobby
enchanted me,
the cappuccinos made
by coke-blazed baristas,
the college girls leaning
into their cool guys,
and me aching
for a girl of my own.

I hunkered down
for the double bill:
Knife in the Water
and *Woman in the Dunes*,
the lush followed by the arid.
I hadn't known that silence
and alienation
were worthy of such attention.

Despite the saxophone track,
a vapor swirling
above the horizon,
the silence was sharper
than the knife.
My fingers spread wide,
daring the blade
as the boat bobbed
in deep water.

And then the small Asian woman.
How else but with mouth open
to watch her sweep
the desert residue
before the sea of sand arrived,
and then after,
the frantic sweeping?

I walked punch-drunk
up the night beach
cackling out loud
about American culture,
its inability to broker silence or
irony.

Against the wall at Kelly's Cove,
half-listening
to the waves crack,
I prayed that living in the salt air
would season me.
Experience was a dark woman
I didn't know
but couldn't stop
lusting after.

THE BARBER

The bald-headed barber on Clement Street
walked out to the sidewalk between customers
and bowed to pedestrians and passing cars.

His shop, an anachronism forty years ago,
had a few homely green chairs,
and a table spread with bawdy magazines.

The clientele was a subsection of the living dead.
Little old men with feathers of angel hair and scalps
that might have been dusted with talc.

Once, in my shaggy youth, I strolled into the shop,
more than likely stoned, in search of a curiosity.
The barber regarded me as a practical joke.

He didn't know what to do with me,
but after a momentary stalemate
we settled on a scissor trim.

I'd have pointed to one of the gleaming heads
in the hairstyle poster,
but they all favored Clark Gable.

The barber could no longer
stand up straight, but he kept
up his quick scissoring,

a driving force of nature,
precise
as a hummingbird's wings.

While he talked baseball,
I tried to imagine
the place in the old days,

with steam and foam
and fogged reflections.
With the razor on the strop.

Beside the barber chair
was an old framed photo
of the barber and his wife.

She had a distant beauty,
he a squint of resignation,
as if he knew

the long scissoring
and silence
that awaited him.

The barber spun me around
so I could see
the back of my neck.

A couple of old guys,
who I reminded myself
had once been children

and lovers
and young fathers,
sat in the green chairs.

I couldn't tell if they'd already
had their hair cut
or were still waiting.

THE OLD COUNTRY

Even as a child
I was fond
of the euphemism.
How it didn't describe
a particular place
with fixed borders
as much as a
prevailing mood,
with a climate
always colder
than anything
I could imagine.

Although a place
impossible to return to
in body,
I rarely heard it
spoken of wistfully.

My grandfather
left in his teens
and spent seventy-five years
trying to forget it.
But Henry,
who had
blue numbers
branded on his arm
six decades ago,
fights to remember it.

After the liberation,
the Czechs gave him
a fat man's suit
and a bicycle.
Can you imagine me,
a hundred and twenty pounds,
in a giant's suit?

I admire the carnival beauty
of the image
until Henry tells how the Russians
took his bike at the Polish border,
and the Poles shot at him
when he finally made it back
to his village.

It is not meant as sacrilege
to suggest that we may
all have a place of horror
and find ourselves,
poor, skeletal creatures
in fat men's suits,
pedaling back to the old country.

NEW YEAR'S DAY

My grandparents, Barnet and Lily Joy,
were married on New Year's Day, 1916.
Both in their thirties, ancient for the time,
they'd courted amid the shops and cafes
of a rebuilt city on the western edge,
my grandfather having left the old country
and his shoeless childhood behind.

The newlyweds honeymooned in Tahoe.
A photo of them, each in huge, hooded furs, survives.
I also have my grandmother's year-long diary,
a small, suede-bound book
that fits in the palm of my hand.
It commences on New Year's Day with a short entry:
Married today. Bliss.
The next day she writes about how handsome
her husband is, how funny he looks in his fur,
how happy she is.

At times in pencil, more often in ink
that still carries its blue sheen,
she notes their daily treats and recreations.
Stopped for hot chocolate on Polk Street.
Abe and Gertie over for cards.
Walked to the Cliff House;
Barnet took a swim in the ocean.
The adventure, begun with the New Year,
settled nicely, it seems, into domestic pleasure.
Early to bed, she writes often,
and then scribbles lines
in an archaic shorthand
that no one alive today can decipher.

I've never been curious
about the sex lives of my grandparents,
who I knew only as feeble,
if loving, creatures.

But on New Year's Day,
nine decades later,
there it is
in coded detail,
in royal blue and faded lead.
A world just begun
and always beginning again.

TWO FATHERS

TWO FATHERS

I. Violinist

I loved most
when you played the Chaconne
of Bach's Partita in D Minor
with your eyes closed.

You learned those
two hundred and fifty-six measures
as a boy but played them for us
as a man, grafting emotion
to Bach's stately perfection.

But I also loved
when you ate onion sandwiches
and fat radishes and hot-mustard slices
of roast tongue.

To work in tux
and cummerbund,
you didn't manage to live
as earthy a life
as you'd have liked.

I think of your ear.
Your perfect pitch.
The squeaks in the street
you'd call B flat.
The E natural farts.
The birdsong.
The fire sirens.
The gloried intonation
in the upper reaches.

Of course, the day to day
was more difficult,
the vagaries of being a father

didn't fit so neatly
into your crowded datebook.
And yet you breathed
a curious tenderness
within the formality
of your absence.

Now that I am old enough to be your father,
there are places I wish I could take you.

II. Bluesman

My father was a bluesman
and I rose every morning
to his rooster call:
Good morning, Blues.
Blues, how do you do?

I'd sit at the table with him
as he yanked out his teeth
and gummed his crispies
in sour mash.

Open the kitchen cupboard
and you'd see dozens of mildewed harps
soaking in yellowed jelly jars,
the reeds warped into half moons,
the unplayed songs rising like vapor.

I remember the weeks the old man
went fetal in his La-Z-Boy, moaning,
Yes, it's a mean old world, baby,
to live in by yourself.

Then he'd leap from the supine
like Little Richard
and be down on all fours
begging for bowls of chili
and cans of Pabst.

I did what I could to comfort my poor mother
when he strutted the house hollering,
I've got a baby she's fine and brown
and what I like about her she's mine all mine.

It was in that house
that I became an atheist,
unwilling to tarry at his shrines
to Robert Johnson, Blind Lemon Jefferson,
or even Sonny Boy.

When he drew out his harp,
I pulled out mine.
We'd blow for hours,
he with the fine hand
of his fat vibrato
fluttering like an open heart,
I going laser, knifing
straight to the marrow.

We traded great, blustery choruses,
furious fours,
and when he'd played himself out,
I'd open it up,
dig through the primal sludge
to a dark growl
that showed the motherfucker some blues
the likes of which he'd never heard.

Trane at the Urinal

All the man did was practice.
For long flights,
he carried a sawed-off broomstick
with bottle caps glued on for keys.

At the Village Vanguard,
when I stand at the urinal,
I think of Trane
planted at the same spot,
with a tenor sax strapped
to his neck.

He'd be running modes,
dark pastures
dense with angular creatures,
fluid as the night.

Feet spread, he'd dig
rich overtones
from the ground
of his tenor, great melons
of sound eclipsing each other.
The man blew chords
from outer space
as he peed.

You've Changed

That sparkle in your eye is gone.

Once, at Keystone Korner,
I heard Dexter Gordon recite
the first line of lyrics so slowly
in his sly, mellifluous voice
that people around me snickered
as if they were listening to a drunk,
and maybe they were.

But then the horn was in his mouth
and he arpeggiated a heroic intro
straight into the flat belly of the ballad,
blowing the blue chorus so gently
you'd have thought he'd taken
the hand of a child
and led her onto the dance floor.

Today I listen to Yusef Lateef's warm, manly tenor,
it, too, religious in its fidelity
to the lyric line.

Maybe everybody after Billie
played it as a tribute to her.
On *Lady in Satin*, her voice shot,
the date mucked up with strings and voices,
she's not out to save anyone,
surely not herself.
The lilt in her voice is now only a hitch,
the longing, languor,
and the changes, the irredeemable losses
all ours.

You're breaking my heart. You've changed.

MONK'S SALT

Thelonious Monk
sprinkles salt
on the back
of his hands
and watches it spill
through his fingers
as they splay
in sharp angles
over the keys.

BIRD OF PARADISE

Of course
I adore
Bird's
open
throated
magisterial
solo
but it's
the lyric
obbligato
the tuneful
underbelly
the selfless
harmonic
empathy
of young
Miles
going
out
that gets me.

VAN MORRISON AT THE GREEK

Forty years ago, as a teen,
I saw Miles Davis impersonate
an ancient horn player here, aiming
his trumpet into the night sky.

Tonight, after the rain,
I wear a floppy felt hat, not unlike Van's—
a baby boomer already boomed,
with grown children and at least
one life left behind.

With Anchor Steam, I cruise the crowd.
So many folks, once raggedy-ass and roused
at antiwar rallies, now affluent.

Before I settle into my hundred-dollar
cheap seat, Van's onstage.
Seven-thirty on the dot,
like he's punching a time card.

At first, even with a fourteen-piece orchestra,
he's nothing more than his own warm-up band,
banging out a forgettable ramble on the keyboard.

But pretty soon he segues into
"It Stoned Me," *stoned me just like Jelly Roll.*
Then an uptown "Moondance,"
with sleek, muted brass,
raising a minimalist skyline.

When he slows it down,
"I Can't Stop Loving You"
becomes aching soul music,
and everyone in the place is left
with the one they can't stop loving.

Years ago, when he was a pretty-boy blond
in a paisley shirt,
I was surprised by his muscularity.
Tonight he's stout and leathery,
obscure as ever,
and it's the man's tenderness
that gets me.

At intermission,
they're out of Anchor Steam.
I climb the muddy hillside
to the top of the theater.
The moon's out.
The wind's still.
The slightest flutter
of eucalyptus leaves.

Before I'm back on my cushion,
the man opens with "Astral Weeks."
The braided beauty
of two acoustic guitars.
If I ventured in the slipstream
Between the viaducts of your dream...

Even at twenty-three, Van could emote
as naturally as breathing.
To never, never, never, never wonder why at all
Never never never never wonder why...
I'm standing beside you.

A vocal dervish.
The sweet, stuttering Irish echo:
All you gotta do is ring a bell.
Step right up, and step right up,
and step right up,
just like a ballerina.

OPEN EYE

OPEN EYE

I only wanted Uncle Vern standing by his new car (a Hudson) on
a clear day. I got him and the car. I also got a bit of Aunt Mary's
laundry and Beau Jack, the dog, peeing on a fence, and a row
of potted tuberous begonias on the porch and seventy-eight trees
and a million pebbles in the driveway and more. It's a generous
medium, photography.

—Lee Friedlander

The history of photography is the history of where to stand,
and I'm wondering where Lee Friedlander's perched
as he snaps Count Basie's band on a bus in 1956.

The musicians are sleeping in rows as far as the eye sees.
Black men with their heads tilted back, mouths open,
a wedding ring on a guy in a sweater vest.
Back a row, a fellow, who I know plays the trombone,
has his head wrapped in a nylon net.

The windows are frosted with grime,
a yellow smear of night lights.
I'm thinking Friedlander's crouched over the aisle,
each foot catching an armrest.

He's not thinking about the men in the frame,
the indignities of their perpetual tour,
or what these hours of lurching slumber mean to them.
To him, the busload of silent hipsters has no resemblance
to a spreading oak, dormant for a night.

He doesn't envision the room they'll play tomorrow night,
or hear the crisp backbeat of the snare and hi-hat,
the lushness of the reeds and brass. Poised in his crouch,
the photographer sees far less than fills his eye.

PAINTERLY

Not being a painter,
I've always wanted to become
a painterly creature,
a long brushstroke of a man,
perfectly witty in tights,
one leg a thin, vertical streak of sienna,
the other a horizontal stripe in umber,
as grounded as an earthen pitcher
painted by Morandi in a rush
of painterly reticence.

Who cares that the pitcher
hasn't poured a glass of water
in an eternity
and that its interest
in the lemon at its side
is scant?

We defer more than we affect.
And what we might have been or done
is as ready a presence
as my painterly double,
beguiling in his glaze
of joy and sorrow.

FAILED GOUACHE

He had hoped
to make a quick painting
of the Holy Spirit,
a fluent gouache on clayboard
without reference
to anything temporal.

It seemed a simple
enough goal,
to achieve a purity
of abstraction
in which God resided,
unburdened by anything earthly.

But weeks went by,
and his studio
filled with clayboard gouaches
riddled with clouds
and handkerchiefs,
wafers and silver rings.

Worst of all, there wasn't
the slightest hint of God anywhere.
Neither His footstep
nor His shadow.

Discouraged, he painted caged quails,
rabbits hanging in the market,
and tureens of mussels,
endless tureens of cackling black shells
in a saffron broth, open wide enough to see
the bone-white meat.

PAINTING BALLPLAYERS

In memory of Andy Nelson (1956-2008)

Baseball was our common language.
As kids, we mainlined it.
In our dreams, ballplayers
forever rounded the bases.
Their stats embroidered our pillow slips
when we laid down our heads.

Decades later, despite the corporate ruination,
we still loved the game.
We belonged to that strange,
if common, breed
who grew up with heroes
we couldn't outgrow as men.

You wanted to paint portraits
of each of the Hall of Famers
in their hometowns.
I counseled a dozen, tops, and call it a day.
No, you said, *I want to leave an image
in all those little towns.*

As it turned out, you painted plenty of Famers,
not necessarily in their hometowns.
I remember your DiMaggio in a tavern
that used his name, north of the Twin Cities.
Your ballplayers tended to have old faces,
and Joe's was arch with purpose.
His fabled nose a garlic clove of glory.

With you gone now, and me back in San Francisco,
I drive around the city
spotting perfect walls for DiMaggio
in the Marin and on Columbus Avenue
in North Beach, blocks from where he grew up.

And yet it's at Kelly's Cove,
along the ocean wall,
with its miles of pocked concrete,
that I see your garden of ballplayers.
Let them face the heaving tumult,
the razored horizon line
at the western edge.

As the waves crash behind you,
the fog, as practiced as a stealthy base stealer,
swoops around your ball cap,
playing tricks with your light.

JUDAS

I love that he did it with a kiss.
The traitor's lips ooze toward Jesus
in generations of Flemish paintings.

I find the story fetching straight through the kiss,
but then it goes to hell. The apostles choose God
and torment Judas as a sacred act.

Returning the silver,
he becomes the sniveling model
for two millennia of Jews.

Humanity, if not God, rises
in the smudged chiaroscuro of Rembrandt's Judas,
wringing his hands in grief.

The fat Pharisees, robed like royals,
are set to send him
to their Abu Ghraib.

I'm with those who believe
that Jesus and Judas were in cahoots,
that the kiss was elegant code.

Who knew a ritual betrayal
would so feed the orthodoxy
that fearmongers on television screens

would violate our dreams with red-faced screams:
Who's taking what's yours?
Who's the Judas?

PROBABILITIES

FURY

Before I blame
everything
on other people's
stupidity and neglect,
and the fact
that so much
that I've expected
and deserved
has not materialized,
I like to put on
a fresh white shirt
and see how quickly
the fury soils it.

SHAME

Far more than opposable thumbs,
shame's the thing that makes us human.

Even if we rub the dog's nose in it,
his shakes and whimpers
echo our crooked sense of justice.

Two short steps from sixty,
I'm as vulnerable to it
as I was as a child, my eyes
hidden behind my forehead.

It has no practical use,
but I've yet to find
a proper way to dispose of it.
It won't compost and doesn't share
the properties of cow dung.
The only thing it fertilizes
is itself.

Sometimes I take a deep breath
and just listen to it:
Don't be a baby.
You should be ashamed of yourself.
Shame on you. Shame.

DELIRIUM

What can I say?
I survive on risotto
and crimini mushrooms
sautéed with capers in the dark.
When morning comes,
I laugh out loud at the buds
of the blood orange tree,
the double white scurry of aphids.
You'd think I was rehearsing
my final delirium, auditioning
my body and soul for science.
I spend whole days reading
and writing poetry—
there's little hope for me.

THE ARGUMENT

We're actually having
an argument,
one of our first,
while crossing the Golden Gate.

You're driving your ex-
boyfriend's Renault
and I'm holding forth
on the virtues
of concision in poetry.
You're not having it.

As you drive
I try to sharpen
my argument,
gazing across
the deep blue
of the bay,
the city
a shimmer
in late afternoon light.

I recite a Creeley poem,
claiming that its elegance
and efficiency
are not unlike
the bridge we're crossing.

You see no virtue
in a *calculation*
crafted of *bloodless lines.*
You argue for expansiveness
as if it's clearly
the more humane approach,
a poetry open-ended,
even messy,
like an actual woman's life.

I roll my eyes
at the idea of such chaos
and discursiveness
but realize I'm losing
the argument.
On top of that
I've fallen in love with you.

Back in the city
our lives expand.
We marry,
move across the country,
raise a family.

As it turns out,
I give up trying
to write brief poems
of elegance and efficiency
in favor of good-sized novels.

It's an old argument,
but I thought you should know—
no matter our estrangement and divorce,
I've begun to see things,
at least these things,
your way.

PROBABILITIES

We are all
betrayer
and betrayed.

We age.

Our beauty
is no longer
what it was.

Our love goes sour.

We lose our way.

ARS POETICA

I wonder how language
so transparent
could ever amount
to anything.
I see a waif in trousers
three sizes too large
who, right before my eyes,
becomes an old-timer
in braided belt
and suspenders.

BENEDICTION

THE NORTH SHORE

The two-dollar cabin, which now goes
for a hundred and fifty bucks a night,
has an opened Gideon Bible
on the table that faces the lake.

Despite the Jesus sign at the entry road
I didn't deliberate. It's high season here,
and driving up the shore
I saw few vacancies.

Also I was drawn to the "resort's" faded sign,
Modern housekeeping cabins,
even though I have no intention
of keeping house.

The Bible is open to Proverbs 15-17.
I'm sure that I am meant to choose one of these
clotted couplets and walk around with it as a portent,
for if ever there was a man open to suggestion, it's me.

I am charmed by the teakettle pattern on the curtains
and the TV with tinfoil on the antenna.
In the bathroom there are two stacks
of washcloths from the Fifties, a cool dozen.

I wonder if a lone man arriving for a single night
is meant to scrub deeply with each cloth
as if, with cheap soap and water,
his sins could be rubbed away.

I wash with a single cloth and
a bar of glycerin I've brought along
and watch the tepid water
swirl down the drain.

We kept house in cabins like this
a little farther up the shore,
the same week every year,
before we had kids and for some time after.

Do you remember the photo you took
of Simone a little more than a year old,
staring at herself in the dime-store mirror
above the kitchen sink?

I've always thought of this as a poet's lake,
maybe because I first heard of it from poets
who'd spent legendary summers here
a generation before we arrived.

Ocean-sized, with a shore as craggy as Maine's,
it leaves salt air and lobsters to the imagination.
A lake too cold to swim in
but perfect for reflection.

Better is a dinner of herbs, where love is,
than a stalled ox and hatred therewith.
In the cabin's tin pots and pans we managed to make
decent meals, with scant herbs and simple food.

We ate gratefully off chipped china on rickety picnic tables.
Now seabirds pick indifferently at cooked green beans
curled into the shape of fried smelt—
my neighbor's leftovers, tossed in a curious act of charity.

I build a small fire,
dine alone on half a sandwich
from a sack, and wonder
what you're eating now.

You used to say that a minute in this lake
would kill a person.
I had no reason to doubt you.
One very warm day you jumped in.

I didn't know whether you were brave or crazy,
but I loved you and kept a nervous eye on my watch.
A minute later, shivering, you scrambled out,
no closer to death than I was.

I don't know if you're allowed
to speak to your former wife
in a poem, but in any case
I am doing it.

Easy to say that for love
I'd dine a lifetime on herbs.
But I say it still
and look out on this lake.

Look out and consider,
as if there were sense to be made,
of how a marriage, once blessed on this shore,
became an ox, stalled in its sad eternity.

SPRING RAIN

I throw on a floppy felt hat
and walk down the street to buy cheese.

Jacket open, I give myself
to the fragrance of orange blossoms,
muted in the warm rain.

The orange tree is one of the legends
of the neighborhood.
In early winter its great globes
will reach the size of grapefruits.

To dispel any confusion of genus
or propriety,
someone will pin to the tree
a hand-written sign:
Please do not steal our oranges.

Now, its wet leaves
curl toward each other
like spooning lovers.

Ig Vella, the old cheese maker,
greets me as if we've been friends
for seventy-five years.

He sits on a crate, in his paper hat,
keeping time with his foot.
Spring rain, he says.
I pick out a block of Dry Jack,
a small tub of cream cheese,
and a hunk of prosciutto.

Ig nods his head
as if he'd placed them in the cooler
just for me.

Last guy, Ig says,
to make a decent prosciutto in North Beach
was your size and half again.
He's been gone for years.

At home,
I toast two heels of sourdough,
spread cream cheese,
and do my best with a dull knife
to carve shavings of prosciutto.

I step outside with my bounty,
one heel for each hand,
and let the rain fall on me.
Surely the giant of North Beach,
the master curer of meats,
must have stood in his doorway
watching the spring rain.

BENEDICTION

For Anton

In the middle of the night,
when your ear infection kicked in,
I'd lift you, mewling, from the crib.
You weren't even a year old.
I held you high against my shoulder
with an arm wrapped around your waist
and another across your back.
We strolled the dark of your small room
until your breathing slipped
into the vapor of night.
One time I joined you,
a sleepwalker
parading in circles
while you, with your perfect weight
and verticality,
turned into a Torah.
It had been decades
since I'd proudly walked the perimeter
of a synagogue
with a Torah in my arms.
But in your room that night
I did it again.
An old man appeared and touched
the kissed fringes of his tallis
to your velvet-wrapped body.
When I laid you in your crib
the scroll opened itself.
With a cracked voice
much like my father's,
I chanted the gnarled words
rising from the parchment.

COFFEE AND FIGS

For Chester and Frances

Nearly a half day gone by
and I'm sated with coffee and figs.
A strong cup of Nicaraguan,
slow-dripped, cream, no sugar.
Aroma and steam, burled flavor
poured into my bloodstream.

I hold a Black Mission by its stem,
twirl it, and admire its uneven swelling,
the shading of its skin
dusted here and there as if by a life
of worry and hard labor.
I break through its skin to bloody flesh.
This is one of the rewards of surviving.

After a dozen Missions
and a second cup of Nicaraguan,
I'm seeing myself as a fig,
well-rounded, sweet-natured, thriving.
I tell myself that there's nothing wrong
with a bit of flattery, that it's just part
of the enterprise,
that a man should play
at least as many tricks on himself
as he plays on others.

By early afternoon I'm freed
of most of my cravings.
I can do without bread and salami.
I can survive without books, or even a woman.
All I want, all I really want,
is coffee and figs.

APRIL FROGS

Tonight I'm strolling through the valley,
and the croaking chatter of the frogs
makes me want to gather my dead
and walk with them
until they tire of my doting.

More than one
whispers nonsense to me.
My reverence is absurd.

Dusk bruises the valley,
leaving a red-honeyed crust,
a few smudged fingers of light.

I tell myself to take
the dead no more seriously
than I take myself.
Their wisdom has its limits.

The frogs, in blessed indifference,
babble as if their long holiday
had just begun.

PRIMEVAL ROCK

It's late spring
before he notices
the pomegranate blossoms
announce themselves
with the aroused red
of a dog's penis,
the firm lips opening,
fuchsia-like, smeared
in a gaudy lipstick.

Older than the apple,
the rough-skinned,
primeval rock,
so beautifully suggested
in the blossom,
posed no temptation in Eden.
It wasn't about to reveal
to just any dumb fools
its tender membranes
and the sweet,
puckering wine
of its seeds.

VALENTINE

It is not only
because you refuse
to wear lipstick

that you are like the blood orange
whose skin resists
the slightest bruise of red.

As with the fruit, my love,
once I've opened you,
all your juicy capillaries

of pulp and pleasure
capture me
for eternity.

MORNING OPERA

The foghorns sound unhappy
with their circumstance.
Buses roar up the street
as if they've taken hostages.
Somehow you are still asleep.
What would happen if I ran a finger
over your lashes?
Say I blew the faintest breath
above your lips,
would they pucker like an urchin?
Your face is almost ready
to open its pockets
to the day.
It is like an opera
five minutes before curtain.
The overture has set its trap,
and the audience,
hushed in hallowed silence,
can't wait for the singing to begin.

SALT AIR

My truant lover has come and it is dark.
I don't ask where she's been.
Her hair's mussed,
her hands closed into fists.
She's not ready to embrace me.
I won't let her know that I worried,
that when the wind came up,
I listened to the howling
and felt it begin inside me.
I offer her coffee, wine, a spot by the fire,
but she stands in the middle of the room,
her striped scarf still knotted.
I think of how long I've known her,
and realize I do not know her.
Slowly, she opens her hands
to show small whelks and augers, tiny urchins.
She slips off her jacket,
holds out an arm toward me.
Come, she says, *see if you can smell
the salt air.*

A Pair of Clydesdales

The small farm down the street raises them,
mighty beasts who have little work.

I see them munching grass in the field.
Tourists wander up from town and snap pictures.

Today the farmer has a pair of young ones
tugging a wagon up the street.

Even as the animals trot slowly toward the cemetery
their feathery fur flies, from hocks to hooves.

The farmer teaches them to stop still on a spot.
They are the deacons of the parade,

and this will be their main trick.
The two horses, unsuspecting, are halted.

The wagon jerks a quiet whiplash.
Huge hooves make single sideways steps.

Heads bob and a shimmying wave runs
through the deep mahogany sheen of the bodies.

The Clydesdales achieve an enviable stillness,
as if they've departed to a corner field of their own.

Clearly, they are not concerned
about becoming ceremonial creatures.

When the farmer jigs them forward, a steaming pile of crap
marks the spot where they stood.

My Father's Insomnia

He looked ancient to me in the dark.
Sitting in his frayed pajamas
in the hall stairway.
Middle of the night, I'd rise to pee
or to spoon myself a bowl of ice cream,
and there he'd be.

He had a favorite spot
huddled under a long window
that my mother had covered in rice paper
to mute a streetlight.

Once I asked what he was doing there.
Worrying, he said.
A strange avocation, it seemed to me,
and an unfortunate time to practice it.
I never asked what troubled him.
I figured his worries and insomnia
belonged to him.

Tonight, in the belly of an old country,
I'm dazed by sleeplessness
and try to picture what's out in the dark:
stones and beauty and sorrow.

By morning, as the cows
sound their mournfulness at waking,
I'm happy to share a stair with my father.
The honey of dawn
through the papered window
lights us up,
a pair of comic cameos.

Birthday in the Mountain Cemetery

New in town, I throw myself a birthday party,
a move designed to spare a bout of solemnity.

Instead of a day barely marked,
another homely gargoyle tacked to the wall,

I ask old friends and a smattering of new
to toast me.

Later, when the party dwindles to less than a dozen,
a carload of poets from west county and a few others,

the poet laureate proposes a hike
to the Mountain Cemetery.

I end up leading a small gang
full with food and wine up the steep street.

Even my mother, dead three years today, joins us.
I decide not to react to her getup,

the large hoop earrings,
the red scarf that looks like it's been half-eaten by a goat.

She is singing to herself,
a three-note song from her childhood.

I leave her and join the poet laureate,
who has the aspect of an Old Testament prophet

without the rage or guile. He also has a new knee
and climbs bravely up the steep hillside.

I love the way the cemetery has become itself,
the outcroppings of rocks and boulders

shifting like megaliths amid
the planted markers.

Both grand and simple lives turned over
by the slow breath of nature.

How strange that here, in the Valley of the Moon,
where grapes and palm trees grow,

family names are branded into rough stone
sepulchres that look like Druids' tombs.

I find solace in seeing the others weave
through the gorgeous garden of stone.

A small band of feral
night creatures.

Even my mother, who's given her song
a buoyant cackle, is panting with joy.

I show my guests the grave of Francis Thornton Sewall,
a native of Gloucester County, Virginia,

born one hundred and fifty-three years
less a day before me.

Time has split his stone into vertical halves
and I am reminded of the Ten Commandments.

I do honor my father and mother in my way,
imagining him, the longtime musician,

luxuriating in the silence
more than anyone would suspect.

And now my mother, who'd hoped to be a diva,
keeps to herself in the night, delighting in her own simple song.

It is almost a pleasure to take her out like this
on my birthday night and let her party
beside the poets, who laugh as if they actually know
something about mortality,

winding their way
through the Mountain Cemetery.

Catherine Durand

Bart Schneider grew up in San Francisco and recently returned to the Bay Area after spending twenty-five years in Minnesota, where he was the founding editor of *Hungry Mind Review* and *Speakeasy*. He is the author of the poetry collection *Water for a Stranger* and four novels, *Blue Bossa*, *Secret Love*, *Beautiful Inez*, and *The Man in the Blizzard*. His new novel, *Nameless Dame*, will be published in the winter of 2012.